HAL LEONARD PIANO REPERTOIRE
Book 4 · *Intermediate*

JOURNEY THROUGH THE CLASSICS

COMPILED AND EDITED BY JENNIFER LINN

Journey Through the Classics is a four-volume piano repertoire series designed to lead students seamlessly from the easiest classics to the intermediate masterworks. The graded pieces are presented in a progressive order and feature a variety of classical favorites essential to any piano student's educational foundation. The authentic repertoire is ideal for auditions and recitals and each book includes a handy reference chart with the key, composer, stylistic period, and challenge elements listed for each piece.

-Jennifer Linn

Dedicated in loving memory to my mother and first teacher,
Geraldine Ruth Ryan Lange.

Cover art: Rose Garden, 1876 (oil on canvas) by Claude Monet (1840-1926)
Private Collection/ Photo © Lefevre Fine Art Ltd., London/ The Bridgeman Art Library
Nationality / copyright status: French / out of copyright
Adaptation by Jen McClellan

ISBN 978-1-4584-1152-5

HAL•LEONARD®
CORPORATION
7777 W. BLUEMOUND RD. P.O. BOX 13819 MILWAUKEE, WI 53213

In Australia Contact:
Hal Leonard Australia Pty. Ltd.
4 Lentara Court
Cheltenham, Victoria, 3192 Australia
Email: ausadmin@halleonard.com.au

Visit Hal Leonard Online at
www.halleonard.com

JOURNEY THROUGH THE CLASSICS:
Book 4 Reference Chart

✔ WHEN COMPLETED	PAGE	TITLE	COMPOSER	ERA	KEY	METER	CHALLENGE ELEMENTS
	4	Little Prelude	Bach, J.S.	Baroque	C	$\frac{4}{4}$	Expanded hand position in broken chords; ornaments
	5	Mazurka	Gurlitt	Romantic	C	$\frac{3}{4}$	Dotted rhythms; chromatic scale
	6	Minuet	Mozart, W.A.	Classical	F	$\frac{3}{4}$	Triplet and 16th note patterns; ornaments
	8	Intrada	Graupner	Baroque	C	$\frac{4}{4}$	Shifting octaves in the LH; Rotation and LH/RH coordination
	10	Sonatina in G	Beethoven	Classical	G	$\frac{4}{4}$	Articulation; Alberti bass and balance between hands
	14	Spinning Song	Ellmenreich	Romantic	F	$\frac{2}{4}$	Legato/staccato coordination between hands; 16th notes and syncopation
	18	Old French Song	Tchaikovsky	Romantic	Gm	$\frac{2}{4}$	Cantabile tone with careful legato fingering; legato/staccato coordination
	20	Gavotte in A Minor	Pachelbel	Baroque	Am	$\frac{4}{4}$	Articulation and ornaments; dynamic contrasts
	20	Gavotte and Variation	Pachelbel	Baroque	Am	$\frac{4}{4}$	Dotted rhythms; articulation and ornaments; 16th note passages
	22	The Merry Farmer	Schumann	Romantic	F	$\frac{4}{4}$	LH melody; voicing and balance between hands
	23	Sonatina in A Minor	Benda	Classical	Am	$\frac{2}{4}$	Shared LH/RH 16th note patterns; syncopation and articulation
	26	Waltz in A Minor	Chopin	Romantic	Am	$\frac{3}{4}$	Waltz bass; balance between hands; pedaling and ornaments
	29	Sonatina Op. 36, No. 2 (III)	Clementi	Classical	G	$\frac{3}{8}$	Legato/staccato coordination between hands; 16th note passages; trill
	34	Invention No. 1	Bach, J.S.	Baroque	C	$\frac{4}{4}$	Coordination of contrapuntal elements and ornaments
	36	By the Spring	Gurlitt	Romantic	A	$\frac{2}{4}$	A major key signature; careful pedal technique and balance between hands
	38	The Avalanche	Heller	Romantic	Am	$\frac{2}{4}$	Vertical reading and rolled chords; quick scale passages divided between hands
	41	Little Prelude in C Minor	Bach, J.S.	Baroque	Cm	$\frac{3}{4}$	Continuous 16th note passages; fingerings in broken chord patterns
	44	Sonatina Op. 55, No. 1 (I)	Kuhlau	Classical	C	$\frac{4}{4}$	Scale passages and Alberti bass; balance between melody and accompaniment
	48	From Foreign Lands and People	Schumann	Romantic	G	$\frac{2}{4}$	Voicing of melody; coordination of accompaniment; dotted versus triplet rhythms
	49	The Storm	Burgmüller	Romantic	Dm	$\frac{4}{4}$	Both hands in bass; rotation of broken octaves; voicing of melody in LH
	52	German Dance	Schubert	Romantic	Am	$\frac{3}{4}$	Careful pedaling; ornaments, voicing, legato octaves in melody
	54	Solfeggietto	Bach, C.P.E.	Baroque	Cm	$\frac{4}{4}$	Even touch tone; coordinating continuous 16th notes shared between hands
	58	To a Wild Rose	MacDowell	Romantic	A	$\frac{2}{4}$	A major key signature; voicing of melody; phrasing and pedaling
	60	Für Elise	Beethoven	Classical	Am	$\frac{3}{8}$	Voicing and balance; pedal technique; 64th notes; repeated notes; chromatic scale

CONTENTS

Little Prelude
BWV 939

Johann Sebastian Bach
(1685–1750)

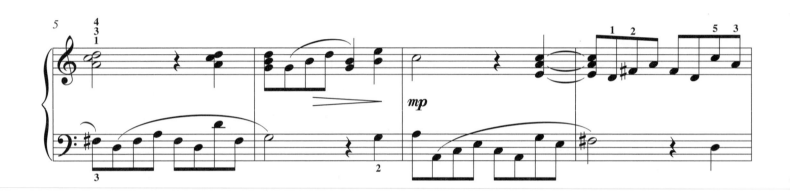

Mazurka

Cornelius Gurlitt
(1820–1901)

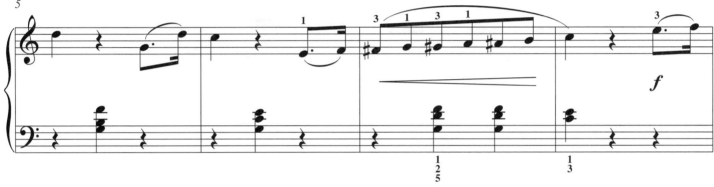

Minuet
KV 5

Wolfgang Amadeus Mozart
(1756–1791)

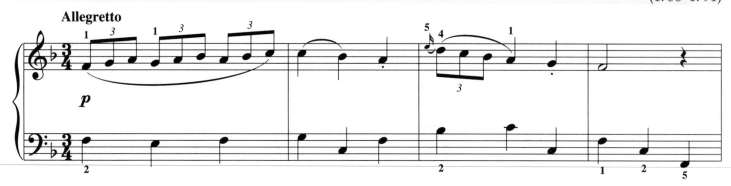

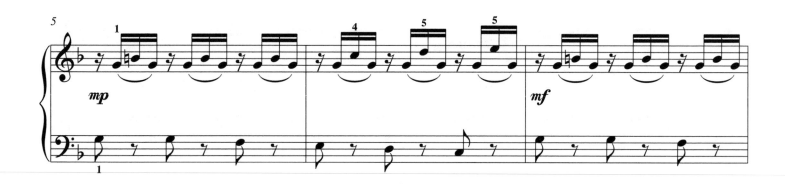

Intrada

Christoph Graupner
(1683–1760)

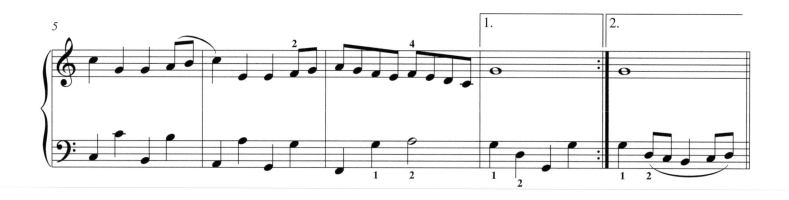

Sonatina in G

Ludwig van Beethoven
(1770–1827)

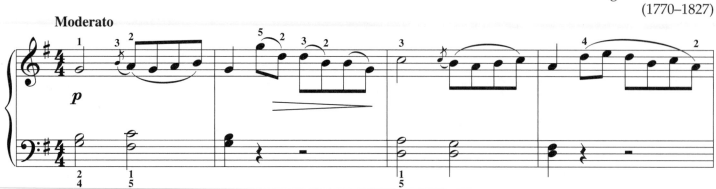

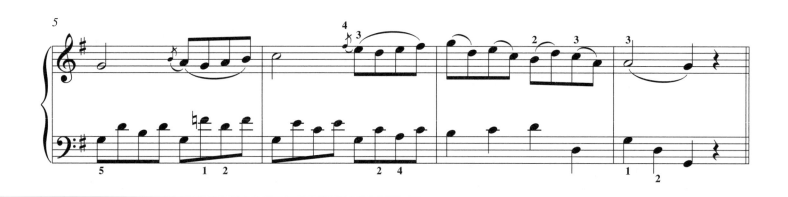

Romanze

Spinning Song

Albert Ellmenreich
(1816–1905)

Old French Song
Op. 39, No. 16

Pyotr Ilyich Tchaikovsky
(1840–1893)

Moderato assai

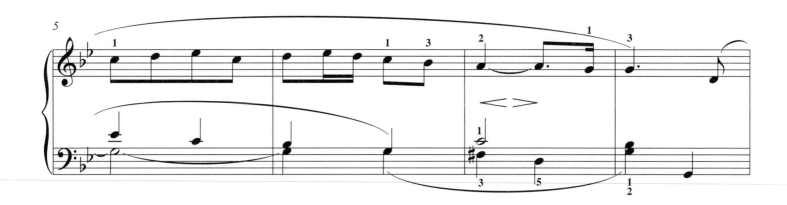

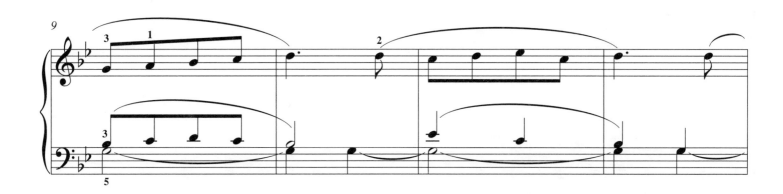

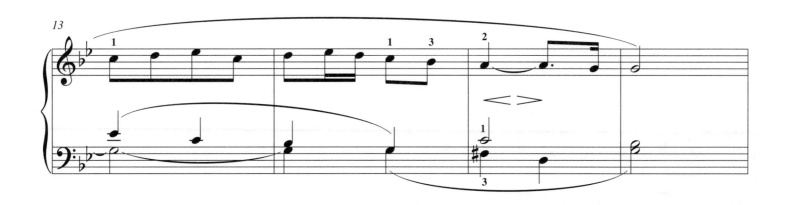

Gavotte in A Minor

Johann Pachelbel
(1653–1706)

Gavotte and Variation

Johann Pachelbel
(1653–1706)

The Merry Farmer
Op. 68, No. 10

Robert Schumann
(1810–1856)

Brisk and lively

Sonatina in A Minor

Georg Anton Benda
(1722–1795)

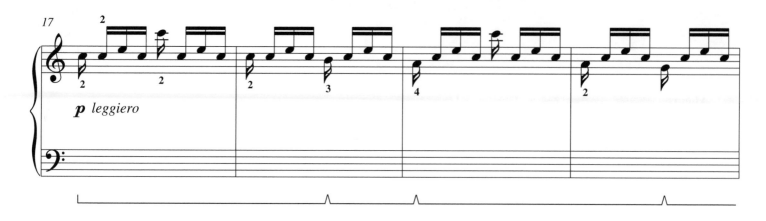

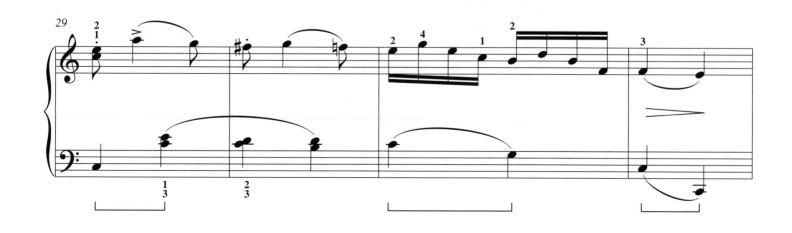

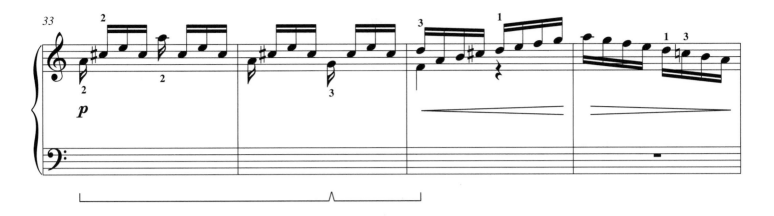

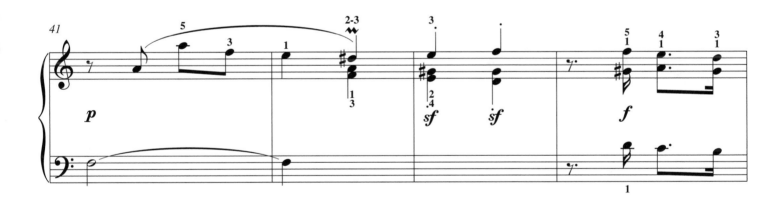

Waltz in A Minor
(Posthumous)

Frédéric Chopin
(1810–1849)

Sonatina
Op. 36, No. 2

III

Muzio Clementi
(1752–1832)

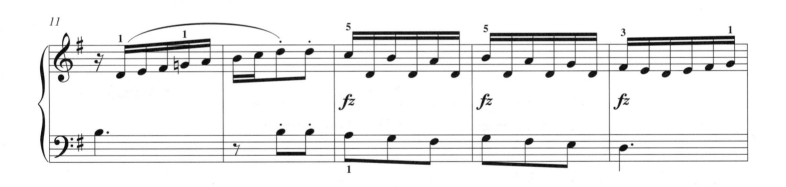

Invention No. 1

Johann Sebastian Bach
(1685-1750)

By the Spring
(Op. 101, No. 5)

Cornelius Gurlitt
(1820-1901)

Moderato, quasi allegretto

The Avalanche
Op. 45, No. 2

Stephen Heller
(1813–1888)

Little Prelude in C Minor
BWV 999

Johann Sebastian Bach
(1685–1750)

Sonatina in C
Op. 55, No. 1

I

Friedrich Kuhlau
(1786–1832)

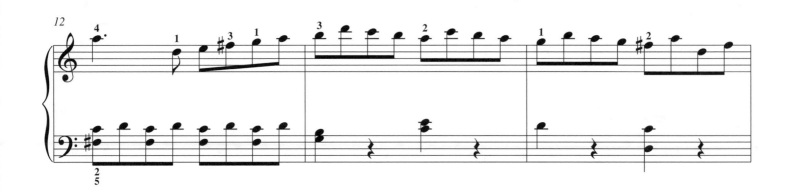

From Foreign Lands and People
Op. 15, No. 1

Robert Schumann
(1810–1856)

The Storm
(Op. 109, No. 13)

Friedrich Burgmüller
(1806–1874)

German Dance
Op. 33, No. 10

Franz Schubert
(1797–1828)

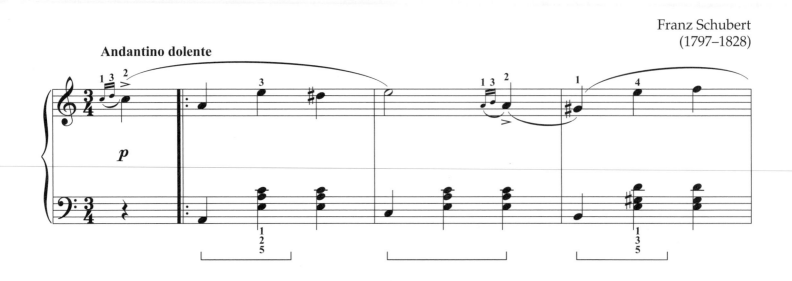

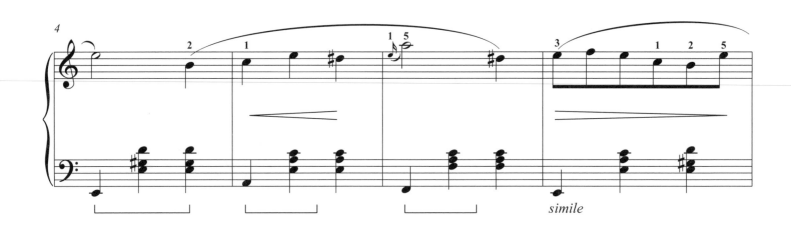

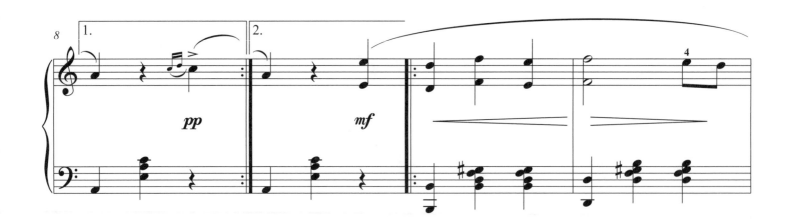

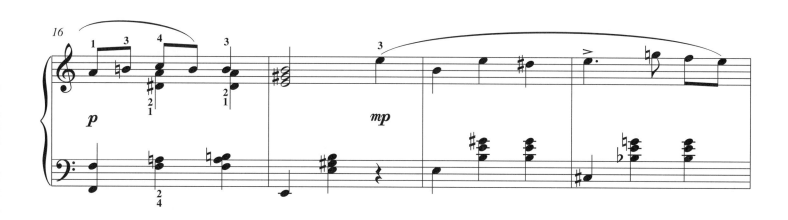

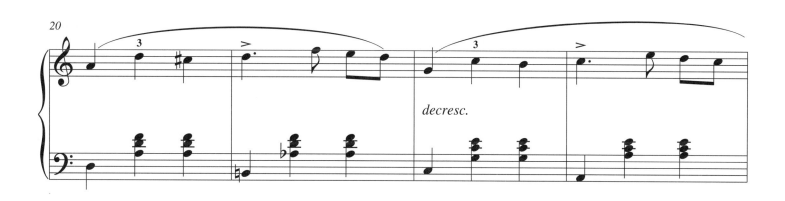

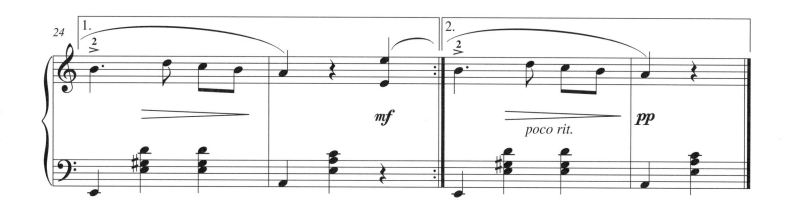

Solfeggietto

Carl Philipp Emanuel Bach
(1714–1788)

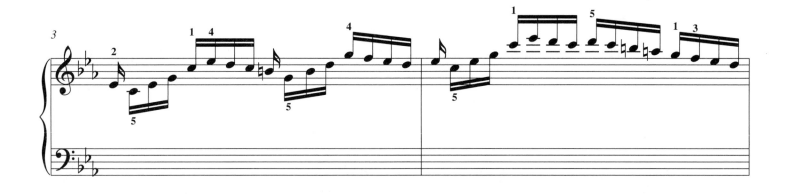

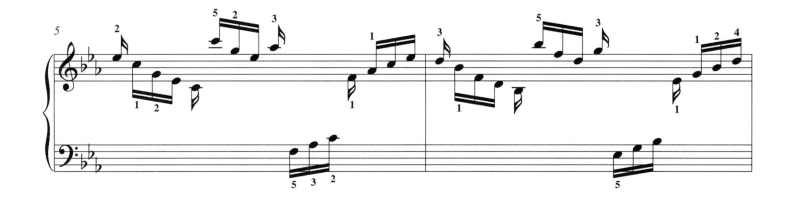

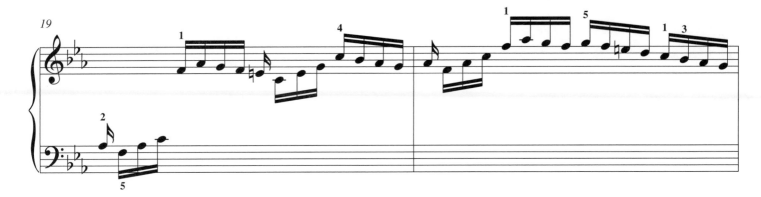

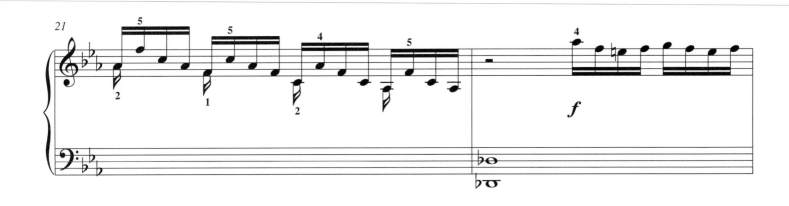

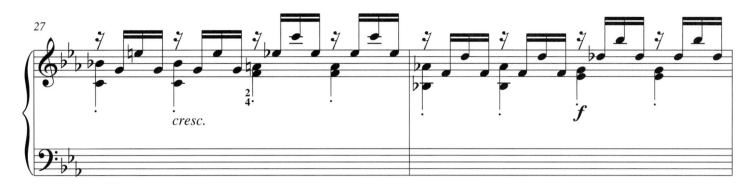

To a Wild Rose
Op. 51, No. 1

Edward MacDowell
(1861–1908)

With simple tenderness

With pedal

Für Elise
WoO 59

Ludwig van Beethoven
(1770-1827)